The Rhythm of Everyday Things

SANDRA SANTIAGO

Copyright © 2014 Sandra Santiago
All rights reserved. No part of this book may be reproduced in any manner without the express written consent of the Publisher, except in the case of brief excerpts in critical reviews or articles. All inquiries should be addressed to: Pandora Lobo Estepario Productions, 1239 N. Greenview Ave. Chicago, IL 60642

ISBN-10: 1940856051
ISBN-13: 978-1-940856-05-6

Library of Congress Control Number: 2014904611

DEDICATION

I dedicate this book to Rosa and Tomás Santiago, to the ancestors who had no voice and who, today, speak through me, and the universal spirits that drive my heart and mind, and my pen.

SANDRA SANTIAGO

Contents

Dancing Women 8
Pelo Malo 10
Piragüero 12
At Maria's Unisex Salon 14
Esperanza Is Hope 16
I am Bat Girl 17
The Rhythm of Everyday Things 18
Gentrification 20
Father's Daughter 22
Five Finger Discount 23
Brown 24
A Pacifist Teacher's Declaration 27
Unspoken Thoughts 29
Storehouse Lamentations 30
Conjuring Woman 31
Third Shift Woman 32
This Land Is Your Land 34
You Call Me Privilege 36
Ode to El Spanglish Poem 38
Upon A Shelf 39
Elixir 40
The Revolutionary's Wife 41
Love Letter to Frida Kahlo: 42
Paper Drinks Ink 44

ACKNOWLEDGMENTS

Thank you to the following individuals and organizations who without their contributions support, and inspiration this book would not have been written: Dr. Yolanda Nieves, YeYe Fun'ke, Yvonne Nieves, Dr. Kelly Norman Ellis, Lisa Alvarado, Diana Pando, Paloma Martinez-Cruz, Crystal Blanton, Linda Garcia Merchant, Dr. Luzma Umpierre, Coya Paz, Robin Fine, Edith Bucio, Harv Roman, Gregory Pickett, Miguel Lopez Lemus, Luis Rodriguez, David Hernandez, Marily Campbell, Lah Tere, Momma Hip Hop Kitchen, Proyecto Latina, Vida Bella Ensemble, Beast Women, Neighborhood Writing Alliance, Guild Complex.

The Rhythm of Everyday Things

DANCING WOMEN

I played Pac-Man and watched
even though I was commanded to
play and stay put.
I waited for Papi
to finish yet another Rum and Coke.
It was always, "After this one."
But, the fifth one came and went.

I watched.
I saw women the color of water
moving in slow motion.
Their cascading, dime-store, rhinestone
earrings bobbed and swayed
in a mid –air dance.
Sideway glances were given.
The graveyard shift began.

The women were an invitation to
a night of charades,
tormenting lonely men who had
finally gotten their
first opportunity in a week,
to spend time in the company
of supernatural ecstasy.
Women swayed their hips to music,
laid their heads on shoulders of men
who smell of stale sweat and
exhaust fumes.

The register chimed
Men bought their partners drinks.
Some women fake sipped,
allowing ice to water down
whiskey into palatable swigs.
The men looked as if they
had never had mothers.
They found confessors
in the dancing women.
Meanwhile, the incessant thoughts
of an endless, naked stupor
tamed their dysfunctions.

THE RHYTHM OF EVERYDAY THINGS

I knew the names
of all the women.
Papi's whores, the dancing women,
Sunshine, Delilah, Jasmine.
Names that brought to mind
picturesque meadows, hills, and flowers
of my Mother Goose book.
Names of flowers
that bloomed then wilted.
Wilted women, withering;
confined within the dimness of
the barroom walls,
 that contained secrets
I should have never known.

PELO MALO

She mumbles
a curse under
her breath.
I watch her
through the mirror.
She pulls the
merciless,
plastic,
instrument of pain
into the tender tresses
she called
Pelo Malo.

Yanking the comb's
sharp teeth
through my head,
numbing my scalp,
tears well up
in the corners of my eyes.
My head
SNAPS BACK
with each stroke.

She,
forcing her will
through my untamable
wild mane;
wrestling with the curl
and the reality
that my herencia
cannot be negated.
It skipped the color
of my skin.
But, permeated up
Through the roots
of the wiry cords
she called
Pelo Malo.

THE RHYTHM OF EVERYDAY THINGS

She combs.
She yanks.
She tugs,
until my Pelo Malo
is transformed
into disentangled,
strands of silk,
saturated in
Johnson's Baby Oil.

SANDRA SANTIAGO

PIRAGÜERO

Standing at his
altar on wheels,
I leer into the cart.
The afternoon sun
streams down,
bathing the syrup's
colors in light.
A bed of glass bottles
hold hues that rival
the neighborhood church's
stained glass windows.

Bottled flavors are
little soldiers donning
plastic spout hat,
positioned at attention,
tamarindo, cherry, piña, coco
grape, orange, and "blue".

I wait for El Piragüero
to minister to me.
Patience is the
virtue of the day.

El Piragüero leans in.
His arms work
the metal blade,
shaving the block of ice,
and forming it into
a conical peak.

THE RHYTHM OF EVERYDAY THINGS

Liberally pouring the syrup,
he saturates the ice
until it comes to
the edge of my cup.
I spill some
onto my shirt.
Then, my hand.
I forego manners as
my tongue races
the stream of sugar
down my arm,
towards my elbow.

This the only time
that Mami doesn't
flail an accusatory finger.
Hot afternoons afford
me the childhood
rite of passage
in sticky fingers,
a stained t-shirt,
and an overflowing piragua cup.

We wait in line
every afternoon,
on the corner
of Kedzie and Cortez
for the Miracle Man,
Saint of the Perpetual Thirst,
El Piragüero.

He makes
the world a better place
one child at a time,
healing the barrio
with sugar and ice.

SANDRA SANTIAGO

AT MARIA'S UNISEX SALON

Snip, snip
the scissors clip off
the curls that swirled
on the girl's head

Once wound
and bound in
rainbow ribbons,
greased,
smoothed,
straightened,
slicked,
softened,
set.

Mami's truth,
it was
a rat's nesting place.
Never mind
the pretty face,
the hair
was a testament
to her disgrace.

But on this day
La nena heard you say
she had nigger hair
one too many times.
She was only nine;
but, pretended
it was fine,
like all the other times

While,
every word
she heard
left a scar
that marred
her brain, her heart.
That was the start of
her withering.

THE RHYTHM OF EVERYDAY THINGS

Clip, clip
that's it
take it all,
take the hair,
make her bare,
she don't care
'cause she knows
she is ugly.

SANDRA SANTIAGO

ESPERANZA IS HOPE

Here, aquí en este lugar,
my name becomes broken glass.
Syllables become shards,
unable to be picked up
by tongues that don't speak
the language of fragility, respect
or self-esteem.

Here, aquí en este lugar,
my name gets tangled like the
knots in my rope.
The sweet, sing-song sounds
of my mother's voice
calling me
become the scrapes
of nails on a chalkboard,
when teacher slices through
the braided tendrils
of syllables in the
 gift bestowed
 by legacy.

Here, aquí en este lugar,
I become
Es-pear-ohn-zah.
and hope means very
little anymore.

I AM BAT GIRL

I am Bat Girl,
Super Niña Murciélago,
montada on my bike,
peddling por ahí,
ignoring las llamadas
de mi Mami.

Wind pushes into me.
I cut through the air.
Soy invencible.
I am invencible.
My wheels don't
touch the road.
The world is
A slow motion
picture show.

I swerve a corner.
Estoy volando,
almost flotando,
faster than Mami's
chancleta in a mid air voyage.
More powerful
than Tio Nito when
he flexes his biceps.
Able to ride over
crookedly cracked sidewalks,
without losing balance.
Gravity becomes a myth
because I am Bat Girl.

I chase myself,
flying to a freedom,
known by only birds and bees.
From everywhere to anywhere
I fly upon the ground

What lies in waiting,
when you are alone?
Running escapes some truths,
but never ends at home.

SANDRA SANTIAGO

THE RHYTHM OF EVERYDAY THINGS

I am from radio rhythms
congas, trumpets, piano
spilling onto the street
from the pounding of bass
as passing cars screech
down the street.
"Amor de Rey,
King Love,"
they call out.

I am from
the dodging of bullets
underneath street lamps,
from open fire hydrants
that relieve the parching
effects of a steamy afternoon.

I am from arroz con gandules,
sopita de leche,
 noches navideñas,
where flashing lights
design a crooked
star in the foggy window.
Falling snow,
whistling winds,
and the warm smells of
an arroz con dulce desert
wrap around me,
reassuring me
like a security blanket.

THE RHYTHM OF EVERYDAY THINGS

I am from amens and hallelujahs,
tambourines and revival tents.
I am from bedtime scriptures
in the language of home.
Scriptures I take to heart,
keep safe in the place
where only Jesus and I
know the real truth
about the grown-up world
that Mami and Papi have tried
so hard to have absolved.

I am from Tomás y Rosa,
Rose and Tommy,
two limbs from different trees
intertwined haphazardly,
From café con leche mornings,
bacalaíto afternoons,
and Ron Bacardi nights.

I am from food stamps,
welfare checks,
and Regan government cheese;
from the toe Papi almost lost to
frostbite in a drunken stupor;
from the gall stone Mami
was rushed off to have removed.

I am from the
occurrences, the memories,
the moments everyone
thought I forgot.
Moments snapped in time,
forever imprinted
inside of me.

SANDRA SANTIAGO

GENTRIFICATION

You the over worked, underpaid,
telenovela, watching,
arroz con gandules cooking,
single mother of one.

You are the harried, hurried,
hopeful full time cashier,
full time student,
no time to breathe,
rushing, working,
always working,
living,
hoping,
dreaming,

You are the street corner rapper,
beat boxer, skate boarder,
undercover graffiti artist.

You are the gang-banging,
pitchfork throwing, street corner soldier;
a legend in your own mind.

You are the mellow dramatic,
hand holding, promise making
high school lovers,
planning on the what if's of tomorrow;
not taking notice of today.

You are the old school B- boy from the hood.
The Café Bustelo drinking,
former factory working, retiree,
reminiscing of how thing "used to be."

You are 50 years of push out, pull in,
Segregate, integrate,
Street riots,
racial unrest,
Sigue pa'lante mi gente
activists.

THE RHYTHM OF EVERYDAY THINGS

You are the
Bomba dancing,
Salsa swinging,
Merengue shaking couples.
Big drum beats pound a rhythm;
extension of my heart beat.
Mi corazón campesino,
Taino- Congo beats that
call out to the Santos
where Ochun and Elegua,
Oya and Yemaya take
physical form
spinning 'round at
Coco's on a Saturday night.

You are the devout Catholic,
7th Day Adventist,
bible thumping Pentecostal,
United Church of Christ,
Non-denominational,
Sunday- best, wearing church goers,
holding on to salvation's golden reigns
while the rest of the world
continues its descend
into some kind of Hell on Earth.

You are the fritura mobile
 cocinero, paletero, piragüero
 hustling to make a day's wage.

You are the here and now.
You are my street.
You are my ' hood
You are the won't be
forced out or evicted.
You are and always will be
Humboldt Park
not Humboldt Heights,
no matter how many
signs say otherwise.

SANDRA SANTIAGO

FATHER'S DAUGHTER

When I walk,
I swagger like him.
No arrogance, vanity
or cockiness.
Just a cool self-assured strut.
Not no unladylike walkin.'
Just a slow movin',
honey sway makin'
men lick they lips
and look long
as I walk on by.

Mami says I got a mean
temperamento like him.
It's the same kind of disposition
that made the carnicero throw
a cleaver and miss Papi's head
by just inches, one time.

I've collected my share of
loves too, just like him.
Mujeriego they called him after
leaving a good woman like mami.
For him, love cost all he was
and never made him free.

I did not learn from his mistakes.
living in casings of loneliness,
searching for some comfort
in the sweet saltiness of skin,
to release me into the world
of nameless yearnings
where whispers and moans
help my soul take flight,
liberating me into life.

THE RHYTHM OF EVERYDAY THINGS

FIVE FINGER DISCOUNT

Una mosca en tu leche.
Una mosca en tu pan.
Si te pica te hace daño
y te puedes enfermar.

                                    Children's rhyme

The rush of adrenaline,
my heart palpitating.
Was it compulsion or obsession?

We were in a recession.
Didn't no one give us nothin.'
It was what you did to get by.
Mami,
la prima,
la Tía.
You do whatcha gotta do,
pero no le digas nada a nadie.
Eso no se menciona.

Childhood specters lingered in
my mother's warnings,
reproaches, and reprimands
Penalties of unnamed
consequences hovered overhead,
Our actions were
dirty truths attracting flies.

SANDRA SANTIAGO

BROWN

Men, relationships and me?
It will always be
a complicated situation
to say the least.
It's a conversation
with no remediation.

You look me
up and down
in disgust.
Thing is,
you look back again,
'cause that disgust
is really a mask of curiosity.
We both know you
want to see what is up
with me.
Tattoos, dark, curly, hair,
broad nose, and other
discernable ethnic traits.

My café con leche,
caramel colored,
mulatta skin
is not dark enough
to be black.
Yet, I'm not
 light enough to be
your painted, porcelain princess.

Call me a chameleon.
I am a shape shifter;
a drifter within
the borders of
your private gauges
 of acceptability.
Controversy surrounds
me because I am brown.

THE RHYTHM OF EVERYDAY THINGS

Brown totes the line
amid the yes and no's
in his mind.
Brown is maybe.
Brown is in between.
In between makes people nervous.
It is purgatory for racial purists

Categorizing,
classifying, and
labeling is oh, so comforting.
As is naming the idiosyncratic,
predictability of my kind.
Yet, complexities arise
when one can't pin point
my ethnic ties.
Guess after guess
on and on you press.
Then, I hear you say,
Oh you're Spanish!

May I remind you
that Spanish is
a language.
I discourage
your improper usage
of the term.

The heavens opened
lifting the hazy veil
of race that covered my face.
My ethnicity is
no longer a mystery.
Suddenly, I have become
a hot to trot Mami
in her Latin state of mind,
shaking it to some internal salsa beat.

I am Carmen Miranda
with maracas in hand.
Legs, breasts, and a big behind,
now you'll make time.
In your mind I have become
a caricature of sexual
conformity and complacency.

Latina,
Latina,
Hispanic,
Spanish,
Spic,
the prostitute or
thick accented maid
in your cops and robber program.
But, don't get me confused
with your Spanish channel,
telenovela, drama-mama.

This face,
this mind,
this body,
are parts of a temple
of power, intellect,
beauty, grace that
will swagger saunter and stride
as I damn well please,
because I am a walking
juxtaposition of what
you want and
what you fear,
a brown woman
in control,
and she is not for sale,
No se vende.

A PACIFIST TEACHER'S DECLARATION

I disagree to the military
showing up to our
elementary school career day.
I am adamant.

Alternatives, you say.
It has become Indoctrination Day,
where the seeds of
military propaganda,
false promises,
 will lead to
these children's demise.

Serve your country.
Be one of the few, the proud.
Be part of something bigger.
The powers that be
deafen our children,
numb their brains,
adding sound tracks
to vignettes that exalt
soldier as action hero,
warrior, savior.

You forget,
our front line soldiers
don't hold college degrees,
can't avoid combat,
don't have daddies to secure
deferment desk jobs.
Options and alternatives
are so easy to offer from
the balcony of privilege.

Ms. Teacher,
that mighty high
seat obscures your sight.
You can't see
what brown mothers
in their tender silence

already know.
Power is held by
a select few,
never listening to reason
This includes you Teacher.

The powers that be
have their own agendas
that discount the
laws of humanity,
justifying murder
by camouflaging it as combat.

UNSPOKEN THOUGHTS

You do not, will not
teach the golden rule to your children.
So why should I?

Your children
spit and laugh, tease and taunt,
yell and screech at my children,
who are schooled in
the teachings of one
very great prophet.

My children who,
turn the other cheek,
share, wait their turn,
say "Please" and "Thank you,"
speaking your
native tongue fluently,
as well our own.

My children are just as
educated, cultivated,
and contaminated
with the values of
this materialistic, capitalistic,
narcissistic, culture.

But, no matter how much
we strive to survive;
no matter what 9-5 job we take,
our presence is still an intrusion.
Is the "American way"
anything more than an illusion?
Pure disillusion,
for those who can
only look in from the
make shift midst
of semi-coexistence
with you my
mono-lingua, anti-immigrant,
English-only, Starbucks sipping,
family values friend.

SANDRA SANTIAGO

STOREHOUSE LAMENTATIONS

Her soul is a well of lamentations
of what was and of what has come to be.
Creases of ageless pain
wrinkle her beautiful,
copper colored,
sun burnt face.
Silver strands of
hair pulled back
in a bun are no longer
as black as the night's
skies of Gualcazar.

Her mind's tapestries
are the remnants
of el campo;
caminadas por la plaza,
rag dolls and lullabies
sung to her.
Then, later sung by her
to her children.

All that is gone now.

She recalls the coarse hands that
took her away and drove her
through midnight roads,
those arteries that led her away
from the valley
of her soul to el norte.

Now she sits in her room,
surrounded by the sounds
of this brave new world,
living within the confines
of this human repository
in the heart of Little Village,
Chicago, Illinois
U.S.A.

CONJURING WOMAN

Conjuring woman
is agua bendita soul,
daughter of diaspora dust,
doesn't not blow in the wind.
She is gathered in molecules
of pressed memories,
conjoined through heart and bone.
You are white doves and black calderos
as the Santos hang from her neck

Conjuring woman
moves in unlit spaces,
argues in the voices of the dead,
wanders in the company of the ancestors,
through the territory of
her name.

Conjuring woman
speaks without moving lips.
Movimiento is language.
El aire becomes a dense,
polyphonic fugue of
ancestral tableaus that trail back
through nude primeval sands,
to the African bush.
The blackness is vacant no more.

Conjuring woman
what can you do with fingertips
in the silent web-weaving of paths
for your children?
Dwelling in mysticism,
the world of the ancients
becomes your own.

SANDRA SANTIAGO

THIRD SHIFT WOMAN

Invisible woman is grey matter.
Moves in shadows,
under the cover of night.
At home the babies
soundly sleep.
She has made sure
to leave bellies fed and cheeks kissed.
She is tempered glass
with backbone of steel.
An equal to any.

Her limbs are a commodity.
Knees bent to scrub floors,
wiping up the drippings of
the day's residue from exhaustion,
dissatisfaction, and sour ambition.

Legs stand for 12 hours
at assembly line work.,
as once nimble fingers become
arthritic appendages.
Language becomes a
barrier, a weapon
for employee compliance.

Her limbs are a commodity.
Calloused hands clean toilets,
cook your food,
scour your pans.
Solid arms carry your babies.
Stooped back toils
to pick your tomatoes,
while her bladder leaks into
her pants and supervisor
gropes a breast.

THE RHYTHM OF EVERYDAY THINGS

Throat empty, void of voice
heart full of fear.
deportation and destruction
of family is not an option.

Her work is a baptism by fire
paying for her children's initiation
into the mainstream so that they
can say, "I too am America."

SANDRA SANTIAGO

THIS LAND IS YOUR LAND

This land is your land.
This land is my land.
But, you don't seem to understand
that we were here first.

We come from those who
speak the world into place.
Brown, skin brown like
the color of earth.
Red, skin red as
the desert sand.

We were here first.

Yet this ceased to be land.
So far from home
yet so near.

First,
Taino,
Chichimeca,
Azteca,
Maya,
Tolteca

Later,
Fulani,
Yoruba,
Ashanti,
Congo,
Mandinka,

We talked among ourselves
and quietly cried through
capture ,survival, and disbursal

So far from home yet so near.
The blood of my veins.
Runs through streams in valleys,
that nourished 1,000
generations of villages.

THE RHYTHM OF EVERYDAY THINGS

The rhythm of that stream
echoes entre the hills,
where birds and tress
once sang to me,
telling me cuentos of
the search for vida y truth.

Those lives have become the anthology
to a history that I now traverse;
distanced, fragmented, uprooted lost.

I am a hollowed coarse carving.
I am diasphoratic nations in self-exile,
carried on waves of
anonymity and yearning.
Ancestor graves cry out,
churning snips of prophecy
in a dangerous language,
saying more of this world
than is contained in any history book.

YOU CALL ME PRIVILEGE

I am the diaspora incarnate.
blood pumps the pain
that ancestors bore
so that I could tell their stories.
they had little
and owned nothing
except collective memories
born of strife,
passed on through
DNA melodies that resonate
motherland heartache
in ears, in mind , in soul

We are the diaspora incarnate
where trapped recallings
emerge from within
the broken bones
of an Alabama coal mine.
Slavery didn't end
with the Emancipation Proclamation
or the ratification of
the 13th Amendment

Blood memory runs deep,
in the skin and sweat of
of a prison chain gang.
each carries a
death sentence by decree
Industrialists replaced
slaves with convicts.
Prison peonage,
Got them hammers swinging high.

Pick axe and chains
are rhythm section.
Voices pound out pain
in the blues of tribulation.
Sound wave chants
keep time,
saving a luckless slinger
from 10 licks by a

THE RHYTHM OF EVERYDAY THINGS

30 inch leather hide
called Black Annie.
Prison guard makes sure
she kisses his back
hard enough for
his skin to leave
 with her

Music is time,
Reminds them that
life moves on
even though the
ridged wilderness
of anguish remains.

You call me privilege,
say I have no business
treading on black memory.
I am the diaspora
incarnate so I am allowed
to tread here.

My grandfather
sang songs growing
cafe and cutting caña.
El canto del Jibaro.
le lo lai le lo lai.
sings the routines of
colonized labor,
in 110 degree sun,
burning abuelito's back is his
stooping, cutting, standing,
cutting, stacking, stooping.
thousands of times a day.

Abueltio did not subdue
the rudeness of el Cañaveral.
But, he laid the tract for my
future cultivation where
I return to the time when
our roots dug into the earth
and became solid
like a sugar cane stalk.

SANDRA SANTIAGO

ODE TO EL SPANGLISH POEM
In honor of Tato Laveria and Luis Piñero

My tongue transforms
the written word
into a sword,
chopiando language,
creating interlingual innovations.

There is insufficiency in English
to describe the diasphoric
condition of my soul.
My words invade el ingles,
as they become the contra
to the prejudice of thick accents
and to the racism against
mispronunciations.

My tongue tastes the words,
mixes the sounds.
Then, rolls the syllables.
The transformation has begun.
The metamorphosis of language
becomes a hybrid bridge
linking two realities that
have never been able
to fully merge.

My words become
seeds that sow our identity,
recreating the foundation
of our existence
conveying our message
from within our souls.

UPON A SHELF

I am no longer owner
of someone else's name
existing on papers that
wrapped the blandness of
my existence.

My back strains,
as I pull myself out from
boxes filled with afterthoughts.
I unpack my soul from limbo.
It is saturated in
new understandings
of old burdens.
The odor of neglect
permeates my skin.

The memories are
artifacts to be shelved
and put away.
I can always
come back to them.
But, I would rather forget
letting them collect dust.

SANDRA SANTIAGO

ELIXIR

Night time is the right time.
Madness drives me.
Or, is it a craving
to seduce you?
Inspiration is the chalice.
Thoughts are wine
dripping onto a waxed floor.
Watch yourself you might slip
on a word or two.

THE REVOLUTIONARY'S WIFE

In the dimness of
the living room
cigarette smoke forms
a rising halo around
the circle of compañeros.
My soul aches
for freedom too.
But, I am banished
to the boiling of rice
and stewing of flesh.
I am encargada of
the shooing away of
the little ones.

They are restless,
baby birds that hover
near their daddies,
picking at particles of sound.
They leave quickly
because the words are
too big for them to digest.

Rebellion is a
forbidden weapon
that I am prohibited
to touch or hold.
My hands are
permitted only babies,
dishes, and brooms.

I am within earshot
and want to holler
to them that I
understand the meaning
of oppression,
that my soul aches
for freedom too.
But today, like always,
I do my que haceres
keeping keep silent
and well-mannered.

SANDRA SANTIAGO

LOVE LETTER TO FRIDA KAHLO:
Retablo in Words

Family outcast.
misunderstood, tortured soul.
Loved, abandoned, strong, needy, human,
injured doe, wounded woman,
constantly searching for the perfect persona.
Like a daily special, one never knew what
was to come from you.

All reveled in your eccentricities.
While, they talked about you
behind your back.
You didn't give a damn!
You drank like a man,
smoked like a man,
cursed like a man,
defied life and death like a man.
You loved like a man
loves a woman,
loves a man.

Querida Frida,
Your canvases were not narcissistic
rants of a spoiled woman.
They were your voice,
mirrors of your alternate reality,
where you suspended your pain,
as the internal and the external were fused.

Art pieced together fragments
of your life in a cross play of
fear, death, love, infidelity,
recollections, regrets,
and transformation.

No matter how independent you were,
you were beholden to your muse.
To live in his shadow was to exist.
To have been anywhere else in
the world would have been hell for you.

THE RHYTHM OF EVERYDAY THINGS

 Ay Frida,
these are not self-inflated
rambling from some wannabe artist,
struggling to find herself.
Mi querida Frida,
the more I run from you the
more I realize I am like you.

SANDRA SANTIAGO

PAPER DRINKS INK

Buildings positioned
in perfect order
are dotted with artificial lights
that mock a twilight sky.
Cars slip through the shadows.
Streetlights glow a muted yellow.
The sparse population below
meanders through
dim corners of night.

No neon lights
to blink brazenly.
No obtrusive sounds
to shatter thoughts.
I am excluded
from the blackness
that hovers outside.
Silence is a malevolent friend
forcing my soul into
writer's compliance

My purging is
a work song rising,
as I pour naked inspiration
onto the page.
My writer's patois
falls like liquid.
Paper drinks ink.

SANDRA SANTIAGO

SANDRA SANTIAGO

Publisher
Pandora lobo estepario Productions
http://www.loboestepario.com/press

www.ingramcontent.com/pod-product-compliance
Lightning Source LLC
Chambersburg PA
CBHW071802040426
42446CB00012B/2679